Kira Obi

KAMAPALA CHUKWUKA

Story Copyright © 2022 Kamapala Chukwuka
Illustrated by Pencil Master Studio
Formatted by zahidul sajib

ISBN 978-1-8382654-1-0

Publisher: Inspired Creative Hub
Contact:
www.inspiredcreativehub.com
hello@inspiredcreativehub.com
kamapalac@gmail.com

Please visit www.kamapalac.com to contact Kamapala for author visits or speaking engagements

This book belongs to:

_____

Our world needs more kindness, thank you for choosing to be one of the people spreading it.

"What would you like to be when you grow up?"

Miss Kaja asked the class.

The room was silent as the children thought about their answers.

Then Bella raised her hand and said, "I want to be a teacher when I grow up!"

Miss Kaja smiled and replied, "That's lovely, Bella."

Jamal shouted, "I want to be a doctor!"

Other answers from the children included: a firefighter, an actor, an astronaut, a mum, a writer, a footballer, a scientist, a musician, a pilot . . .

The children went on, one after the other. . . except Obi.

Miss Kaja walked up to him with a reassuring smile and asked, "What about you, Obi?

What would you like to be?"

"I . . . "Obi whispered, "I would like to be kind." Miss Kaja beamed. "That's very sweet, Obi!" "My grandma says I can be anything I want to be but the most important thing is to be kind," Obi added.

"Indeed, Obi!" answered Miss Kaja.

"We all should try to be kind, shouldn't we class?

"Yes, Miss Kaja!" the children answered loudly.

Obi loved being kind!

His mum often said he had a *big heart* because he always tried his best to put others first.

Obi also loved having a *big heart* and making others happy.

His dad often reminded him that one good way to be kind is by using your manners to say 'Please' and 'Thank you

Obi always used his manners. At the supermarket he thanked the check-out lady while his mum was on her phone.

Obi was kind thoughtful and considerate of others.

But being kind wasn't always so easy. Sometimes Obi had to be really brave to show kindness.

Like the day Tim made fun of Raj's turban. Obi was scared to speak up in case Tim made fun of him too.

But Obi knew his big heart would be sad if he didn't speak up. Luckily, Tim didn't make a fuss and apologised to Raj straight away.

Being kind sometimes meant being

Patient.

When Kayla jumped ahead of Obi in the lunch queue, he didn't make a big deal out of it.

The teachers at school loved Obi because he was always ready and willing to help.

For example, Obi was right there when Miss Kaja needed help to set up for lessons.

Another time, he helped Mr. Jackson tidy up after arts and crafts.

Being kind made Obi happy!
However, sometimes it meant

Sacrifice.

One time mum made a tasty mango pie. There was one piece left and Obi wanted it, but he knew his little brother did too, so he let him have it.

It was almost Kindness Week at Obi's school.

That week, the children and teachers would perform random acts of kindness both in school and outside of school.

The children would each fill out a journal describing the random acts of kindness they had performed.

Obi was nervous about what he should write in his journal during Kindness Week. He was known to be kind, thoughtful and used his manners already.

What acts of kindness could he perform to fill his journal for seven whole days?

He couldn't write: On the first day, I said 'Please' and 'Thank you.' Nope, that certainly wouldn't be good enough!

It would have to be much bigger and kinder.

"I'm worried about Kindness Week." exclaimed Obi.

"There's no need to worry" his mum replied. "Just remember what Grandma always tells us, that being kind isn't hard. All it takes is doing little unexpected things, to show that you care."

"Remember that no act of kindness is ever too small to make a difference. Tiny as they may seem, they all add up to make a huge impact." His dad added.

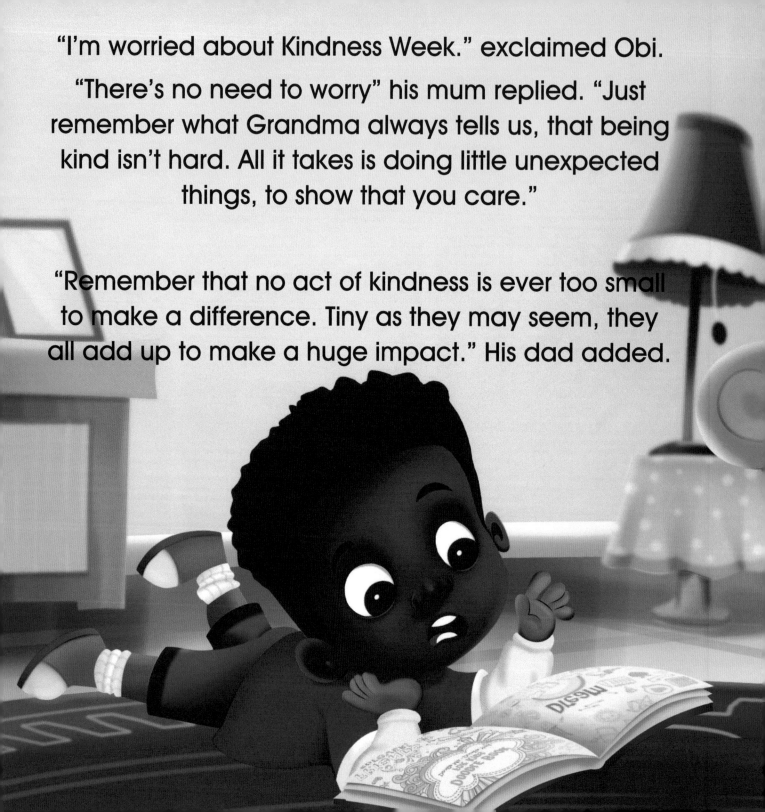

Obi thanked his parents, who had helped him realise what course of action he should take. He would do what he already did best:

Share

his big heart wherever he went!

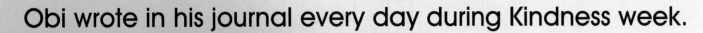

Obi wrote in his journal every day during Kindness week.

This is what he wrote.

At the supermarket, I gave the sales assistant a big smile and a cheerful "Thank you" when she checked out our shopping

At the dentist, I held the door for an old lady and her cute Labrador dog.

I brought freshly-baked cookies to Mike, the homeless man who sits by the station entrance.

I made a bird feeder and filled it with water and yummy seeds for the birds to enjoy.

I gathered up litter in the park, helping to make it look sparkling clean.

I made my bed and put away my toys before Mum asked.

I wrote a 'Thank You' note to Tim, the friendly postman, for bringing us the mail.

Before long, Kindness Week had come to an end!

The children had all done an amazing job with their Kindness Journals! They each received a prize as a reward.

Ms. Kaja was very proud of the children. And she had one more act of kindness of her own in store for the kids . . .

They'd all be going on a trip to see the big circus that was coming to town!

The End

Hey friends, my mum says performing an act of kindness is doing something nice for someone without expecting anything in return.

I love spreading kindness, hope you do too.

There are several examples of simple acts of kindness performed throughout this book.

Here is a table with more examples.
Will you choose a few to perform and write down in your kindness journal?
Great, thanks!

Offer to play with the new kid or someone who's all on their own	Write your teacher a note or a poem about why you like them	Hang up someone's coat if it's fallen off its peg	Choose an extra item to donate to a food bank when you go shopping	Do a sponsored bake/walk/run and raise money for charity
Plant something - tree/flower	Sign up to Post Pals and write a letter to a child who's ill in hospital	Try to walk/cycle to school more to help cut down pollution	Sort out your old toys to donate to a local charity	Pick up litter from the school playground/parks
Put out water and seeds for birds	Create a gratitude jar at school or at home	Help out with chores like loading the dishwasher, clearing up after dinner, tidying up your toys	Write an apology note to say sorry to a friend if you've hurt their feelings	Write to your MP about something that could be better in your area

To send a child who is ill in hospital a letter, ask your adult to visit https://www.postpals.co.uk/

Please can you share your gratitude journals and kindness ideas with me?
Email address : kamapalac@gmail.com
Website : www.kamapalac.com

Kindness Journal

Name : _____

Monday

Tuesday

Wednesday

Thursday

Friday

Saturday

Sunday

Well done on completing your journal!
I'm proud of you and I bet you are proud of yourself too.

No act of kindness is too small to make a difference

Dear Reader,

Kind Obi is a book I really enjoyed writing. I hope it came across and you loved reading it too.

Would you be ever so kind to leave me a review on Amazon & consider sharing with others.

Could you share a photo or 2 on social media & tag me? I love seeing your photos & reading your words. They inspire me to keep sharing my gift of writing.

I would be delighted to see all your beautiful colouring pages so please do share with me as well.

You can find me on Instagram & Facebook as @kamapala_c

Visit my website www.kamapalac.com for fun activities, inspiration & updates

I'm available for Author visits,
Library/group zoom calls + visits

I'm also available for motivational talks on confidence contact me :
kamapalac@gmail.com

Kamapala Chukwuka is a wife & mum of 3 boys, author and founder of a small creative digital marketing agency inspiredcreativehub.com

She writes diverse children's books with a strong focus on black character leads.

She writes these books to inspire little black/brown boys and girls to love themselves and be confident in who they are.

She feels representation in children's literature is very important as it offers ALL children variety in what they read and promotes acceptance of others.

Her hobbies are spending quality time with her family, hosting friends, writing, and being in the outdoors.

OTHER BOOKS BY THE AUTHOR

MUMMY'S LOVE FOR YOU WILL ALWAYS BE

AMA'S GIFT

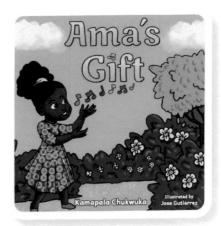

Printed in Great Britain
by Amazon

87740520R00025